Analogy Adventure

Creating and Solving Analogies • Grades 4 – 8

Written by Linda Schwartz
Illustrated by Beverly Armstrong

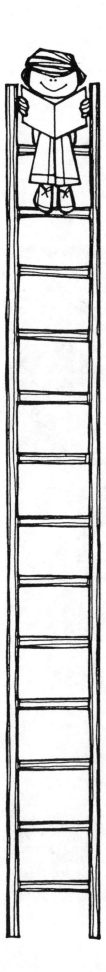

The Learning Works

Edited by Sherri M. Butterfield

The purchase of this book entitles the individual classroom teacher to reproduce copies for use in the classroom.

To the Teacher

Lead your students on an exciting word journey. Take them on an **Analogy Adventure** in which they learn to analyze, solve, and write analogies.

An analogy is a relationship between a pair of words which serves as the basis for the creation of another pair. If the analogy has been completed correctly, the words in the second pair have the same relationship to each other as do the words in the first pair. Because analogies are "word puzzles," working with them gives today's students some much-needed practice in analyzing relationships while strengthening their vocabularies and increasing their creativity.

The twenty-five pages of analogy exercises in this book have high-interest adventure themes. These exercises include analogies based on relationships involving words that name animal groups or offspring; words that are antonyms, synonyms, or homophones; and words that name individual members of a larger group or recognized parts of a whole. The exercises are arranged so that both the vocabulary they contain and the concepts on which they are based become progressively more difficult. The analogies are written in each of the two formats currently being used on standardized tests so that students will become familiar with both.

In addition to the exercises and an answer key, this book contains a number of special features. Among them are word lists students can use when writing their own analogies, a score chart on which individual students can keep track of their progress, a reproducible award with which teachers can recognize achievement, and Analogy Whizo, an original game that can be played for analogy practice by a small group of students or by an entire class.

Contents

All About Analogies

What Is an Analogy?

An **analogy** is a relationship between one pair of words or terms that serves as the basis for the creation of another pair of words or terms. If the analogy has been completed correctly, the terms in the second pair have the same relationship to each other as do the terms in the first pair.

What Are These Relationships?

The relationships that form the basis for the completion of analogies vary from one analogy to another. For example, terms in the first pair may be **synonyms**. That is, they may have the same meaning. They may be **antonyms**, terms that have opposite meanings. Or they may be **homophones**, words that have the same sound but have different spellings and different meanings. One term in the pair may name the **group** of which the other term is a **member**. Or one term may name a **whole** of which the other term is a recognized **part**.

But, no matter what the relationship between the terms in the first pair, the terms in the second pair must be related to each other in *exactly* the same way for the analogy to be correct. In other words, if the terms in the first pair are synonyms and the terms in the second pair are antonyms, no analogy exists among the four terms. Their relationship is *not* **analogous**.

How Do You Write an Analogy?

Analogies are usually written in the form

<u>Happy</u> is to <u>sad</u> as <u>generous</u> is to <u>selfish</u>.

To shorten this form, a single colon is sometimes used in place of the words *is to*, and a double colon is used in place of the word *as*, to separate the two pairs that make up the analogy.

<u>happy</u> : <u>sad</u> : : <u>generous</u> : <u>selfish</u>

How Do You Complete an Analogy?

Read the first pair of terms and think about the relationship between them. It might help to ask yourself these questions: Are the terms synonyms or antonyms? Are they homophones? Is one a recognized part of the other or a member of the group named by the other?

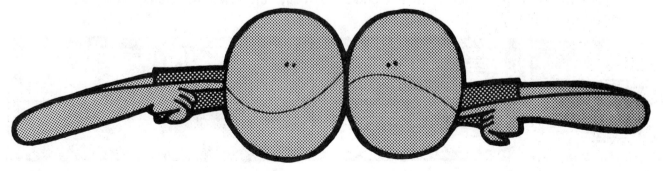

All About Analogies
(continued)

Example: purchase : buy : : throw : _____
           a. ball   c. throe
           b. catch   d. toss

In this example, the words underline purchase and buy are **synonyms.** They *mean the same thing*. Which word among the four lettered answer choices means the same as throw? You throw a ball, but ball does not mean the same thing as throw. Catch means the opposite of throw. Throe sounds like throw but has a completely different meaning. Only toss is a **synonym** for throw. Thus, d. toss is the term that correctly completes the analogy, and you should underline it.

Example: nose : head : : finger : _____
           a. foot   c. nail
           b. hand   d. toe

In this example, a nose *is found on a* head. Thus, a nose is a **recognized part of** a head. Where is a finger found? On a hand. Thus, b. hand correctly completes the analogy. Fingers are not found on feet, nails, or toes.

Example: oriole : bird : : elm : _____
           a. fish   c. leaf
           b. flower   d. tree

In this example, an oriole *is a kind of* bird. Thus, bird names the **group** of which oriole is a **member**. What word names the group of which elm is a member? An elm is not a fish or a flower. An elm has leaves, but leaf does not name the group of which elm is a member. An elm is a tree. Thus, d. tree is the term that correctly completes the analogy, and you should underline it.

Example: pin : cushion : : letter : _____
           a. box   c. mail
           b. envelope   d. sew

In this example, a cushion *holds a* pin. What holds a letter? A box could hold a letter, but would not normally be used for this purpose. You mail a letter, but a mail does not hold a letter. Although pins are used to sew, sew has little or nothing to do with letter. Among the lettered answer choices, b. envelope is the only one that names something that normally *holds a* letter. Thus, this choice correctly completes the analogy, and you should underline it.

   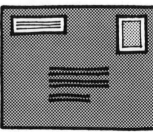

Analogy Practice

Synonyms	are words that mean the same thing, such as <u>false</u> and <u>untrue</u> or <u>easy</u> and <u>simple</u>.
Antonyms	are words that mean opposite things, such as <u>start</u> and <u>stop</u> or <u>in</u> and <u>out</u>.
Homophones	are words that sound the same but are spelled differently and mean different things. For example, <u>made</u> and <u>maid</u> are homophones.

Example: narrow : thin : : tiny : _____

_____

     a. tall   c. little
     b. timid   d. giant

In what way are the words <u>narrow</u> and <u>thin</u> related? They are **synonyms**. Write this word on the line below the analogy. Which of the lettered answer choices is a synonym for <u>tiny</u>? Underline it. Answer choices a. tall and d. giant are antonyms for the word <u>tiny</u>. Answer choice b. timid is not related to the word <u>tiny</u> in any of the ways listed in the box. Thus, answer choice c. little correctly completes the analogy.

For practice, complete the following analogies. First, decide if the relationship between the words in the first pair is that they are **synonyms**, **antonyms**, or **homophones**. Write one of these three words on the line below the analogy. Then, look at the first word in the second pair and decide which one of the lettered answer choices is related to it in the same way. Underline this answer choice.

1. forward : backward : : smart : _____

_____

     a. alert   c. hurt
     b. bright   d. stupid

2. dull : sharp : : beautiful : _____

_____

     a. blade   c. handsome
     b. cut   d. ugly

3. blew : blue : : flower : _____

_____

     a. flour   c. rose
     b. horn   d. sky

4. late : tardy : : bashful : _____

_____

     a. brash   c. prompt
     b. early   d. shy

FORWARD   BACKWARD

More Analogy Practice

On page 7, you completed analogies in which the words were **synonyms**, **antonyms**, or **homophones**. Below are some examples of other relationships you will discover during the course of your analogy adventures. In each one, <u>underline</u> the word that best completes the analogy.

Recognized part of a whole
toe : foot : : finger : hand

1. leg : slacks : : sleeve : _____
   a. arm   c. pocket
   b. button   d. shirt

Individual member of a larger group
reptile : turtle : : bird : swan

2. insect : grasshopper : : fish : _____
   a. aquarium   c. salmon
   b. bug   d. swim

An exotic, unusual, or specific shade of a basic color
azure : blue : : ruby : red

3. rhodamine : red : : lapis lazuli : _____
   a. blue   c. purple
   b. green   d. yellow

The name given to an animal group
swarm : bees : : covey : quail

4. gaggle: geese : : rafter : _____
   a. ceiling   c. turkeys
   b. monkeys   d. wolves

The name given to the offspring of a particular animal
cub : bear : : kitten : cat

5. gosling : goose : : fry : _____
   a. egg   c. gaggle
   b. fish   d. roe

Tools and the occupations or trades with which they are customarily associated
wrench : plumber : : plow : farmer

6. microscope : scientist : : telescope : _____
   a. astronomer   c. observatory
   b. laboratory   d. planets

Words that name male and female counterparts
gander : goose : : rooster : hen

7. bull : cow : : stallion : _____
   a. cattle   c. mare
   b. horse   d. steer

If you cannot identify the relationship between the words or terms in a pair, look them up in a dictionary. You may learn about a definition of which you have been unaware and, in doing so, discover how the words are related. In the two examples below, you will probably find several words with which you are unfamiliar. Look up these words. Identify the relationship between the words in the first pair. Write the word that names this relationship on the line. Then, <u>underline</u> the word that best completes the analogy.

8. boredom : ennui : : jail : _____

   _____

   a. cage   c. prison
   b. excitement   d. prisoner

9. onymous : anonymous : : approbatory: ____

   _____

   a. approving   c. identified
   b. disapproving   d. unknown

Balloon Bonanza

Instructions: <u>Underline</u> the word that best completes the analogy.

1. up : down : : hot : _____

   a. fire   c. warm
   b. cold   d. stove

2. balloon : rubber : : shoe : _____

   a. foot   c. leather
   b. boot   d. sock

3. rise : fall : : float : _____

   a. sink   c. parade
   b. autumn   d. soar

4. air : gas : : water : _____

   a. wet   c. melt
   b. shower   d. liquid

5. wind : air : : current : _____

   a. berry   c. blow
   b. water   d. event

6. blue : sky : : green : _____

   a. cloud   c. grass
   b. sun   d. color

7. swim : water : : fly : _____

   a. air   c. fish
   b. bird   d. wing

8. east : west : : south : _____

   a. down   c. north
   b. low   d. pole

9. tie : knot : : fasten : _____

   a. close   c. key
   b. latch   d. tether

10. pennant : flag : : jacket : _____

   a. cold   c. warm
   b. banner   d. coat

Jungle Journey

Instructions: <u>Underline</u> the word that best completes the analogy.

1. trip : journey : : car : _____
   - a. travel
   - b. automobile
   - c. caravan
   - d. road

2. rabbit : hop : : snake : _____
   - a. slither
   - b. reptile
   - c. rattle
   - d. rodent

3. forest : tree : : garden : _____
   - a. jungle
   - b. mow
   - c. flower
   - d. green

4. leg : chair : : leaf : _____
   - a. green
   - b. trunk
   - c. photosynthesis
   - d. tree

5. tropic : hot : : arctic : _____
   - a. ice
   - b. cold
   - c. north
   - d. steam

6. coconut : tree : : grape : _____
   - a. raisin
   - b. wine
   - c. vine
   - d. fruit

7. leader : guide : : writer : _____
   - a. author
   - b. safari
   - c. tour
   - d. story

8. eyes : see : : ears : _____
   - a. sight
   - b. hear
   - c. noise
   - d. nose

9. beat : drum : : blow : _____
   - a. air
   - b. sound
   - c. music
   - d. whistle

10. parrot : jungle : : camel : _____
    - a. dessert
    - b. mammal
    - c. desert
    - d. bird

Food Fantasy

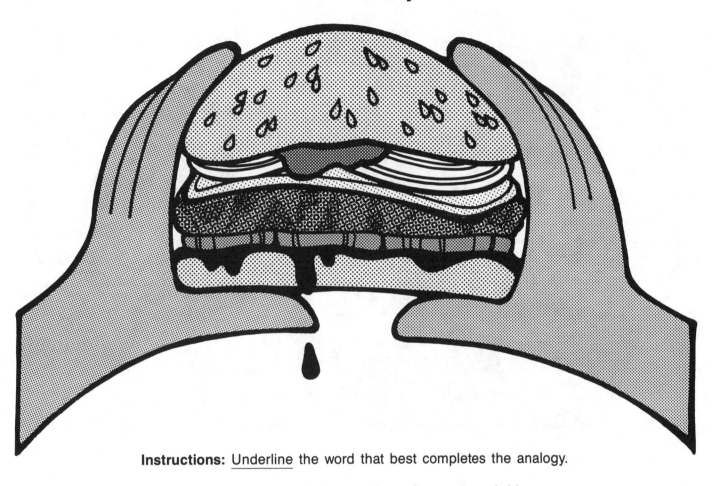

Instructions: <u>Underline</u> the word that best completes the analogy.

1. lemon : sour : : candy : _____
   a. sweet   c. cane
   b. chocolate   d. eat

2. fruit : apple : : flower : _____
   a. blossom   c. pretty
   b. daisy   d. smell

3. money : bank : : milk : _____
   a. cream   c. pitcher
   b. chocolate   d. coffee

4. peanut butter : jelly : : spaghetti : _____
   a. food   c. noodle
   b. meatballs   d. pasta

5. ate : eight : : mail : _____
   a. letter   c. man
   b. male   d. stamp

6. salt : pepper : : bride : _____
   a. ceremony   c. wedding
   b. groom   d. woman

7. beef : meat : : asparagus : _____
   a. eat   c. meet
   b. fruit   d. vegetable

8. cheese : milk : : ketchup : _____
   a. bottle   c. mustard
   b. hamburger   d. tomato

9. taffy : candy : : rose : _____
   a. bush   c. smell
   b. flower   d. thorn

10. cinnamon : spice : : tea : _____
   a. beverage   c. bag
   b. coffee   d. pot

Safari Sampler

Instructions: <u>Underline</u> the word that best completes the analogy.

1. hunt : seek : : dense : _____
   a. find   c. tents
   b. hide   d. thick

2. guide : lead : : beg : _____
   a. big   c. seek
   b. plead   d. tell

3. giraffe : calf : : ostrich : _____
   a. bunny   c. cub
   b. chick   d. gosling

4. gorilla : guerrilla : : prey : _____
   a. ape   c. food
   b. chimpanzee   d. pray

5. lead : follow : : advance : _____
   a. adjust   c. guide
   b. go   d. retreat

6. colt : zebra : : joey : _____
   a. Joseph   c. pouch
   b. kangaroo   d. stripes

7. beetle : insect : : piranha : _____
   a. bug   c. scary
   b. fish   d. small

8. fur : cats : : scales : _____
   a. birds   c. reptiles
   b. pounds   d. weight

9. pride : lion : : colony : _____
   a. flag   c. proud
   b. monkey   d. rabbit

10. canteen : water : : hamper : _____
    a. basket   c. drink
    b. clothes   d. hinder

Name _____

Farm Fun

Instructions: <u>Underline</u> the word that best completes the analogy.

1. sheep : lamb : : bear : _____
   a. cub   c. kit
   b. kid   d. zoo

2. fish : scales : : bird : _____
   a. eagle   c. fur
   b. feathers   d. song

3. kid : goat : : fawn: _____
   a. bear   c. deer
   b. beaver   d. rabbit

4. feet : foot : : geese : _____
   a. claw   c. gaggle
   b. honk   d. goose

5. brood : birds : : litter : _____
   a. dogs   c. lizards
   b. fishes   d. trash

6. chicken : chick : : duck : _____
   a. bird   c. duckling
   b. drake   d. goose

7. dog : bark : : rooster : _____
   a. chicken   c. hen
   b. crow   d. sound

8. ewe : you : : do : _____
   a. dew   c. does
   b. did   d. done

9. fish : fin : : bird : _____
   a. beak   c. scale
   b. feather   d. wing

10. children : child : : oxen : _____
    a. animal   c. ox
    b. mammal   d. oxens

River Raft Revenge

Instructions: <u>Underline</u> the word that best completes the analogy.

1. river : stream : : mountain : _____

    a. hill   c. peak
    b. top   d. valley

2. raft : water : : glider : _____

    a. high   c. stream
    b. log   d. air

3. rapid : slow : : shallow : _____

    a. water   c. lazy
    b. deep   d. fast

4. dangerous : safe : : male : _____

    a. female   c. lad
    b. mail   d. hazardous

5. clock : time : : thermometer : _____

    a. scale   c. temperature
    b. water   d. event

6. salmon : fish : : magpie : _____

    a. dessert   c. bird
    b. plant   d. reptile

7. give : take : : wet : _____

    a. rain   c. puddle
    b. dry   d. water

8. swarm : bees : : school : _____

    a. class   c. learn
    b. fish   d. building

9. feather : soft : : rock : _____

    a. pillow   c. stone
    b. garden   d. hard

10. gills : fishes : : lungs : _____

    a. mammals   c. air
    b. oxygen   d. water

Name _____

Sports Spectacular

Instructions: <u>Underline</u> the word that best completes the analogy.

1. touchdown : football : : goal : _____

   a. baseball   c. soccer
   b. golf   d. tennis

2. player : team : : actor : _____

   a. cast   c. group
   b. game   d. stage

3. sport : basketball : : fish : _____

   a. reptile   c. tuna
   b. school   d. water

4. bat : baseball : : stick : _____

   a. football   c. soccer
   b. hockey   d. tennis

5. court : tennis : : ring : _____

   a. boxing   c. finger
   b. circle   d. jewelry

6. club : golf : : racket : _____

   a. net   c. tennis
   b. soccer   d. volleyball

7. ball : bawl : : boll : _____

   a. baseball   c. cotton
   b. bowl   d. weevil

8. run : race : : play : _____

   a. actor   c. game
   b. athlete   d. stage

9. win : lose : : happy : _____

   a. birthday   c. sad
   b. frown   d. smile

10. golf : course : : bowl : _____

    a. alley   c. caddy
    b. ball   d. club

Mountain Mania

Instructions: Underline the word that best completes the analogy.

1. high : low : : many : _____
   a. count   c. number
   b. few   d. people

2. mountain : peak : : path : _____
   a. crest   c. top
   b. snow   d. trail

3. climb : ascend : : hike : _____
   a. descend   c. tramp
   b. rappel   d. up

4. volcano : lava : : geyser : _____
   a. hot   c. spring
   b. mountain   d. water

5. peak : peek : : vale : _____
   a. look   c. valley
   b. top   d. veil

6. fall : drop : : cut : _____
   a. autumn   c. scissors
   b. knife   d. trim

7. danger : risk : : happen : _____
   a. happy   c. hurry
   b. hardy   d. occur

8. geologist : rocks : : botanist : _____
   a. animals   c. plants
   b. oil   d. scientist

9. incline : slope : : cavern : _____
   a. cave   c. hill
   b. crag   d. mesa

10. dig : scoop : : arrive : _____
    a. aim   c. come
    b. arrest   d. leave

Museum Mystery

Instructions: <u>Underline</u> the word that best completes the analogy.

1. architect : buildings : : composer : _____
   a. ballet   c. paintings
   b. music   d. sculpture

2. guard : protect : : steal : _____
   a. patrol   c. swipe
   b. security   d. watch

3. arrive : depart : : appear : _____
   a. come   c. look
   b. emerge   d. vanish

4. exhibit : display : : value : _____
   a. admission   c. show
   b. pay   d. worth

5. brush : artist : : baton : _____
   a. conductor   c. stroke
   b. stick   d. surgeon

6. indigo : blue : : crimson : _____
   a. crime   c. red
   b. criminal   d. yellow

7. gilt : guilt : : palate : _____
   a. gold   c. mouth
   b. innocence   d. palette

8. work : problem : : solve : _____
   a. dissolve   c. play
   b. mystery   d. solution

9. pepper : spice : : turquoise : _____
   a. aqua   c. silver
   b. color   d. tourniquet

10. diamond : gem : : atlas : _____
    a. book   c. ring
    b. maps   d. stone

Pirate Peril

Instructions: Underline the word that best completes the analogy.

1. peril : danger : : promise : _____
   a. lie   c. truth
   b. pledge   d. wise

2. sail : ship : : drive : _____
   a. car   c. wave
   b. road   d. way

3. pirate : robber : : journalist : _____
   a. column   c. typewriter
   b. newspaper   d. writer

4. chest : trunk : : sack : _____
   a. bag   c. football
   b. can   d. grocery

5. map : chart : : treasure : _____
   a. atlas   c. cherish
   b. bury   d. riches

6. back : front : : stern : _____
   a. bow   c. face
   b. deck   d. severe

7. flag : pole : : sail : _____
   a. banner   c. mast
   b. cloth   d. sale

8. aisle : isle : : naval : _____
   a. island   c. navy
   b. navel   d. orange

9. captain : crew : : leader : _____
   a. boat   c. group
   b. follower   d. sailor

10. stars : stripes : : skull : _____
    a. brain   c. flag
    b. crossbones   d. head

Aerospace Adventure

Instructions: <u>Underline</u> the term that best completes the analogy.

1. pilot : airplane : : driver : _____
   a. astronaut   c. spaceship
   b. car   d. train

2. arrival : departure : : beginning : _____
   a. coming   c. opening
   b. end   d. start

3. plane : plain : : pedal : _____
   a. bicycle   c. peddle
   b. flat   d. push

4. launch : start : : warn : _____
   a. blast-off   c. rocket
   b. caution   d. safety

5. ignite : extinguish : : flexible : _____
   a. burn   c. floppy
   b. fire   d. rigid

6. sun : star : : earth : _____
   a. meteor   c. planet
   b. moon   d. satellite

7. calm : stormy : : tranquil :_____
   a. cool   c. quiet
   b. peaceful   d. turbulent

8. altitude : altimeter : : distance : _____
   a. high   c. odometer
   b. miles   d. speedometer

9. take off : land : : embark : _____
   a. bark   c. tree
   b. disembark   d. water

10. squadron : airplane : : flock : _____
    a. bee   c. fly
    b. chicken   d. wing

Carnival Caper

Instructions: <u>Underline</u> the word that best completes the analogy.

1. carnival : fair : : holiday : _____
   - a. food
   - b. party
   - c. treat
   - d. vacation

2. caper : prank : : joke : _____
   - a. comedian
   - b. laugh
   - c. tell
   - d. trick

3. mask : face : : costume : _____
   - a. actor
   - b. body
   - c. Halloween
   - d. witch

4. giggle : laugh : : frisky : _____
   - a. easy
   - b. happy
   - c. playful
   - d. sad

5. cotton candy : eat : : pink lemonade : __
   - a. drink
   - b. pink
   - c. straw
   - d. sweet

6. booth : stand : : wagon : _____
   - a. cart
   - b. food
   - c. gate
   - d. wheel

7. spin : wheel : : toss : _____
   - a. catch
   - b. rings
   - c. roll
   - d. throw

8. win : prize : : buy : _____
   - a. lose
   - b. pay
   - c. purchase
   - d. souvenir

9. band : banned : : knight : _____
   - a. castle
   - b. chivalry
   - c. maiden
   - d. night

10. march : parade : : sing : _____
    - a. choir
    - b. float
    - c. month
    - d. sang

Monster Mash

Instructions: <u>Underline</u> the word that best completes the analogy.

1. mash : squash : : mix : _____
   - a. mend
   - b. cook
   - c. cut
   - d. blend

2. vampire : bat : : killer : _____
   - a. wing
   - b. whale
   - c. fang
   - d. mammal

3. enormous : huge : : tiny : _____
   - a. large
   - b. big
   - c. small
   - d. hug

4. man : men : : mouse : _____
   - a. mice
   - b. shower
   - c. rodent
   - d. liquid

5. scare : frighten : : calm : _____
   - a. alarm
   - b. spook
   - c. startle
   - d. soothe

6. howl : wolf : : roar : _____
   - a. lamb
   - b. lion
   - c. boar
   - d. roof

7. claw : cat : : toenail : _____
   - a. paw
   - b. foot
   - c. human
   - d. finger

8. dragon : monster : : castle : _____
   - a. king
   - b. tail
   - c. wall
   - d. building

9. strong : weak : : brave : _____
   - a. cowardly
   - b. courage
   - c. bold
   - d. fear

10. boot : foot : : glove : _____
    - a. mitten
    - b. hand
    - c. baseball
    - d. leather

Scuba Scare

Instructions: <u>Underline</u> the word that best completes the analogy.

1. fish : shark : : bird : _____

   a. feather   c. pelican
   b. fly   d. wing

2. sea : see : : beach : _____

   a. beech   c. sand
   b. ocean   d. surf

3. clear : cloudy : : clean : _____

   a. dirty   c. sky
   b. soap   d. wash

4. murky : dark : : hidden : _____

   a. apparent   c. inky
   b. concealed   d. open

5. sand : bar : : coral : _____

   a. drift   c. sharp
   b. reef   d. tear

6. harpoon : spear : : snorkel : _____

   a. boat   c. knife
   b. fish   d. tube

7. Hawaii : island : : Australia : _____

   a. kangaroo   c. England
   b. continent   d. peninsula

8. eight : octopus : : two : _____

   a. biped   c. one
   b. mollusk   d. too

9. exterior : interior : : flimsy : _____

   a. outside   c. solid
   b. shaky   d. weak

10. depth : height : : doubt : _____

    a. apex   c. up
    b. belief   d. wonder

Rodeo Roundup

Instructions: <u>Underline</u> the word that best completes the analogy.

1. rooster : hen : : bull : _____

   a. elephant   c. cow
   b. dog   d. animal

2. bronco : horse : : lariat : _____

   a. pony   c. saddle
   b. ride   d. rope

3. wild : tame : : strong : _____

   a. weak   c. force
   b. powerful   d. flame

4. horns : cattle : : antlers : _____

   a. horses   c. music
   b. deer   d. sharp

5. hat : head : : chaps : _____

   a. arms   c. hands
   b. feet   d. legs

6. buggy : carriage : : corral : _____

   a. cart   c. pen
   b. livestock   d. wagon

7. wrench : plumber : : plow : _____

   a. harvest   c. rake
   b. crops   d. farmer

8. gait : gate : : main : _____

   a. door   c. mane
   b. fence   d. street

9. cowboy : ranch : : scientist : _____

   a. doctor   c. laboratory
   b. experiment d. scientific

10. cattle : herd : : wolf : _____

    a. barn   c. flock
    b. den   d. pack

Gold Rush

Instructions: Underline the word that best completes the analogy.

1. ore : oar : : carat : _____
   a. carrot   c. row
   b. gold   d. vegetable

2. rush : hurry : : adjust : _____
   a. fast   c. prod
   b. fix   d. turn

3. prospector : miner : : hermit : _____
   a. crab   c. mine
   b. explorer   d. recluse

4. vein : vane : : lode : _____
   a. blood   c. load
   b. carry   d. weather

5. grub : food : : dough : _____
   a. bread   c. pizza
   b. money   d. rummage

6. metal : mettle : : wade : _____
   a. iron   c. water
   b. medal   d. weighed

7. day : week : : quart : _____
   a. foot   c. liquid
   b. gallon   d. pound

8. glitter : sparkle : : gloss : _____
   a. dull   c. gold
   b. glossary   d. luster

9. foolish : wise : : near : _____
   a. close   c. narrow
   b. far   d. next

10. genuine : real : : fake : _____
    a. bonus   c. doubt
    b. counterfeit   d. worth

Explore Galore

Instructions: <u>Underline</u> the term that best completes the analogy.

1. seek : search : : explore : _____

   a. claim   c. send
   b. probe   d. travel

2. huge : vast : : galore : _____

   a. abundant   c. meager
   b. bargains   d. space

3. cartographer : maps : : lithographer : __

   a. calligraphy   c. prints
   b. carts   d. stones

4. buoy : boy : : fore : _____

   a. aft   c. girl
   b. for   d. life preserver

5. Old World : Europe : : New World : ____

   a. Africa   c. Australia
   b. Asia   d. North America

6. Florida : peninsula : : Panama : _____

   a. continent   c. isthmus
   b. island   d. river

7. keen : sharp : : moist : _____

   a. damp   c. dry
   b. desert   d. messy

8. barter : trade : : mutiny : _____

   a. bounty   c. merchant
   b. launch   d. rebellion

9. canoe : paddles : : galley : _____

   a. Indians   c. oars
   b. kitchen   d. ship

10. route : course : : cargo : _____

   a. carstop   c. path
   b. freight   d. road

Gone Fishing

Instructions: Underline the word that best completes the analogy.

1. fish : barracuda : : bird : _____

   a. dove   c. flight
   b. feather   d. peace

2. deep : shallow : : fresh : _____

   a. new   c. sassy
   b. rude   d. stale

3. inch : yard : : centimeter : _____

   a. foot   c. meter
   b. liter   d. mile

4. emu : robin : : mackerel : _____

   a. bird   c. trout
   b. fish   d. whippet

5. catch : miss : : exact : _____

   a. ball   c. precise
   b. fish   d. vague

6. front : back : : slow : _____

   a. crawl   c. snail
   b. fast   d. stop

7. ambitious : lazy : : busy : _____

   a. bee   c. idle
   b. harried   d. rushed

8. worm : bait : : rice : _____

   a. chicken   c. food
   b. earth   d. paddy

9. fisherman : boat : : fire fighter : _____

   a. hook   c. net
   b. hose   d. truck

10. tease : taunt : : petty : _____

   a. peculiar   c. sticky
   b. pretty   d. trivial

Jam Session

Instructions: <u>Underline</u> the word that best completes the analogy.

1. woodwind : oboe : : brass : _____
   a. bronze   c. piano
   b. flute   d. trumpet

2. berry : jam : : cucumber : _____
   a. bush   c. squash
   b. pickle   d. vine

3. accordion : violin : : polka : _____
   a. dance   c. music
   b. duet   d. waltz

4. sharp : flat : : up : _____
   a. down   c. high
   b. dull   d. over

5. sound : ear : : odor : _____
   a. mouth   c. perfume
   b. nose   d. smell

6. loud : soft : : rude : _____
   a. coarse   c. polite
   b. manners   d. vulgar

7. tune : melody : : beat : _____
   a. eggs   c. song
   b. rhythm   d. strike

8. blew : blue : : chord : _____
   a. color   c. harmony
   b. cord   d. notes

9. high : low : : treble : _____
   a. band   c. three
   b. bass   d. tremble

10. audio : hear : : video : _____
    a. ear   c. see
    b. eye   d. sound

Taste Treat

Instructions: <u>Underline</u> the pair of terms that best completes the analogy.

1. meringue : egg : :
   - a. ambrosia : coconut
   - b. cake : cookie
   - c. custard : pudding
   - d. sage : thyme

2. marlin : grunion : :
   - a. beetle : insect
   - b. maple : sugar
   - c. toucan : oriole
   - d. tuna : fish

3. whip : cream : :
   - a. boil : steam
   - b. dice : cut
   - c. knead : dough
   - d. saute : fry

4. teaspoon : tablespoon : :
   - a. acre : land
   - b. ounce : cup
   - c. ton : pound
   - d. year : week

5. devil : egg : :
   - a. chicken : rooster
   - b. poach : fish
   - c. scramble : whip
   - d. spud : potato

6. rooster : hen : :
   - a. bull : elephant
   - b. filly : mare
   - c. drake : duck
   - d. ewe : sow

7. shell : egg : :
   - a. banana : fruit
   - b. bird : nest
   - c. seed : apple
   - d. skin : peach

8. singe : burn : :
   - a. obvious : clear
   - b. scale : weigh
   - c. single : several
   - d. solitary : numerous

9. saffron : topaz : :
   - a. beige : khaki
   - b. diamond : hard
   - c. red : green
   - d. ring : jewelry

10. Rome : Italy : :
    - a. London : Paris
    - b. Madrid : Spain
    - c. Norway : Sweden
    - d. pizza : sauce

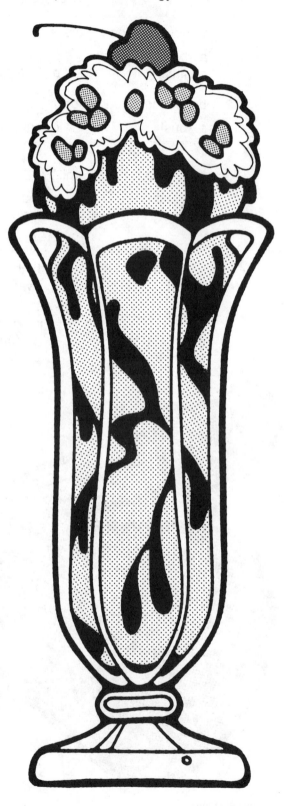

Amazing Amusements

Instructions: <u>Underline</u> the pair of terms that best completes the analogy.

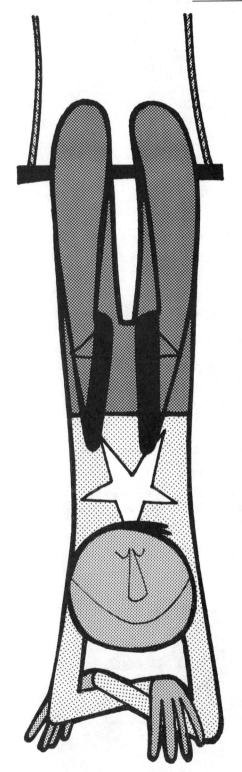

1. swing : playground : :
   a. Ferris wheel : carnival   c. pool : water
   b. ocean : sea   d. slide : movie

2. read : magazine : :
   a. book : newspaper   c. music : concert
   b. listen : tape   d. taste : sweet

3. Tarzan : Jane : :
   a. Detroit : Chicago   c. Hansel : Gretel
   b. forest : jungle   d. queen : king

4. banjo : strum : :
   a. bugle : blow   c. pedal : bike
   b. organ : pipe   d. sing : melody

5. stars : astronomer : :
   a. doctor : nurse   c. mankind : anthropologist
   b. fossils : dinosaur   d. podiatrist : nose

6. paddle : Ping-pong
   a. baseball : strike   c. court : basketball
   b. bow : archery   d. soccer : guard

7. rivalry : competition : :
   a. acceptance : rejection   c. implication : suggestion
   b. confident : insecure   d. important : insignificant

8. terrarium : plant : :
   a. aquarium : fish   c. flower : fruit
   b. bird : cage   d. soil : earth

9. ornithologist : birds : :
   a. cardiologist : cards   c. ivy : plant
   b. entomologist : insects   d. stamp : collector

10. duet : two : :
    a. many : few   c. song : dance
    b. solo : one   d. quartet : three

Science Sensation

Instructions: <u>Underline</u> the pair of terms that best completes the analogy.

1. rhinoceros : calf : :

   a. antelope : kid
   b. bark : dog
   c. colt : filly
   d. tiger : lion

2. sensation : wonder : :

   a. amusement : entertainment
   b. feeling : happy
   c. science : scientist
   d. sense : cents

3. solve : problem : :

   a. answer : key
   b. arithmetic : math
   c. experiment : laboratory
   d. test : hypothesis

4. volt : electricity : :

   a. battery : cell
   b. bulb : light
   c. decibel : sound
   d. switch : current

5. cirrus : cloud : :

   a. aster : rose
   b. circus : clown
   c. viola : instrument
   d. weather : storm

6. circle : radius : :

   a. angle : square
   b. measurement : ruler
   c. point : line
   d. wheel : spoke

7. stable : horse : :

   a. brood : chick
   b. cow : graze
   c. house : home
   d. sty : pig

8. Fahrenheit : temperature : :

   a. Edison : light bulb
   b. Franklin : lightning
   c. Richter : earthquake
   d. Steinway : piano

9. test : experiment : :

   a. chemistry : physics
   b. learn : know
   c. method : technique
   d. observation : research

10. geologist : rocks : :

    a. florist : flowers
    b. meteorologist : meteors
    c. meteorologist : weather
    d. zoologist : zoos

Anatomy Ambush

Instructions: <u>Underline</u> the pair of terms that best completes the analogy.

1. surprise : ambush : :
   - a. accept : refuse
   - b. advance : retreat
   - c. attack : assault
   - d. find : lose

2. knee : leg : :
   - a. ankle : foot
   - b. elbow : arm
   - c. thumb : finger
   - d. wrist : hand

3. eye : wink : :
   - a. cry : tears
   - b. ear : head
   - c. fingers : snap
   - d. lash : brow

4. hair : head : :
   - a. bald : skin
   - b. cap : hat
   - c. hand : glove
   - d. nail : finger

5. pupil : eye : :
   - a. drum : ear
   - b. learn : see
   - c. open : close
   - d. student : teacher

6. heel : foot : :
   - a. arm : leg
   - b. nail : cut
   - c. nape : neck
   - d. sock : shoe

7. scapula : shoulder : :
   - a. femur : leg
   - b. finger : nail
   - c. skeleton : bone
   - d. tibia : skull

8. lungs : air : :
   - a. gills : water
   - b. inhale : exhale
   - c. mouth : throat
   - d. oxygen : gas

9. expand : contract : :
   - a. chase : pursue
   - b. relax : tighten
   - c. run : exercise
   - d. strong : muscle

10. chew : mouth : :
    - a. chest : lungs
    - b. digest : stomach
    - c. ribs : cage
    - d. teeth : tongue

Sly Spy

Instructions: <u>Underline</u> the word pair that best completes the analogy.

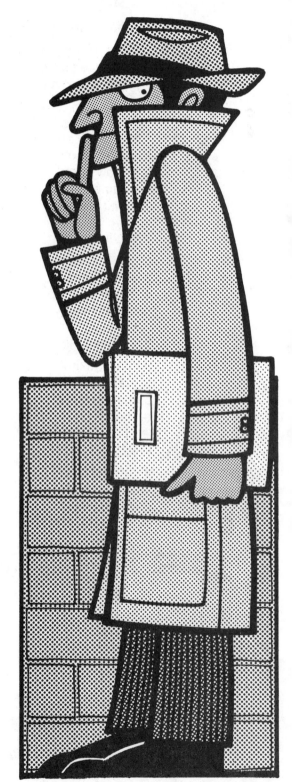

1. sly : clever : :
    a. cunning : clumsy
    b. furtive : stealthy
    c. meat : cleaver
    d. sane : crazy

2. spy : agent : :
    a. actor : play
    b. editor : manuscript
    c. president : secretary
    d. sleuth : investigator

3. secret : covert : :
    a. hidden : exposed
    b. open : overt
    c. public : private
    d. secrete : culvert

4. paper : parchment : :
    a. insect : beetle
    b. pencil : pen
    c. scissors : blade
    d. tree : grass

5. sedan : limousine : :
    a. auto : driver
    b. horse : trailer
    c. truck : wheel
    d. yacht : sloop

6. fear : fright : :
    a. exhausted : rested
    b. scene : steal
    c. truce : war
    d. zeal : fervor

7. gun : weapon : :
    a. bow : arrow
    b. hammer : nail
    c. knife : blade
    d. screwdriver : tool

8. intimidate : frighten : :
    a. general : specific
    b. pale : bright
    c. sparse : sparrow
    d. unify : unite

9. negotiate : bargain : :
    a. assemble : adjourn
    b. insert : delete
    c. previous : prior
    d. sale : sail

10. capture : release : :
    a. apprehend : catch
    b. free : emancipate
    c. imprison : liberate
    d. captive : prisoner

Daredevil Dynamo

Instructions: <u>Underline</u> the word pair that best completes the analogy.

1. daring : adventurous : :
   - a. bold : timid
   - b. cautious : reckless
   - c. foolhardy : rash
   - d. strong : weak

2. deed : feat : :
   - a. calm : storm
   - b. dead : feet
   - c. import : export
   - d. trick : stunt

3. zephyr : breeze : :
   - a. cyclone : typhoon
   - b. rain : sun
   - c. tropical : climate
   - d. weather : forecast

4. aviator : aviatrix : :
   - a. aircraft : plane
   - b. braver : bravest
   - c. hero : heroine
   - d. pilot : copilot

5. feet : altitude : :
   - a. atmosphere : air
   - b. fathom : depth
   - c. low : high
   - d. slow : fast

6. explore : investigate : :
   - a. invite : invitation
   - b. prolong : extend
   - c. antique : modern
   - d. cocoon : caterpillar

7. agile : clumsy : :
   - a. ballerina : graceful
   - b. brave : cowardly
   - c. sagacious : wise
   - d. shrewd : clever

8. vermilion : red : :
   - a. gold : silver
   - b. orange : apple
   - c. rainbow : cloud
   - d. russet : brown

9. silly : frivolous : :
   - a. ambitious : lofty
   - b. complex : simple
   - c. logical : confusing
   - d. meddle : medal

10. decade : ten : :
    - a. century : hundred
    - b. deck : card
    - c. even : odd
    - d. inch : yard

Create Your Own Analogies

Instructions: Now that you have had practice in completing analogies, try creating some of your own. For ideas, use the word lists on pages 36–41, as well as a dictionary, thesaurus, or other similar reference materials.

Analogies Based on Synonyms or Antonyms

Examples: hardy : strong : : sensible : wise
heavy : light : : common : unique

1. _____ : _____ : : _____ : _____
2. _____ : _____ : : _____ : _____
3. _____ : _____ : : _____ : _____
4. _____ : _____ : : _____ : _____
5. _____ : _____ : : _____ : _____
6. _____ : _____ : : _____ : _____

Analogies Based on Animal Offspring or Animal Groups

Examples: tiger : cub : : deer : fawn
colony : rabbits : : flock : birds

1. _____ : _____ : : _____ : _____
2. _____ : _____ : : _____ : _____
3. _____ : _____ : : _____ : _____
4. _____ : _____ : : _____ : _____
5. _____ : _____ : : _____ : _____
6. _____ : _____ : : _____ : _____

Create Your Own Analogies
(continued)

Instructions: On the lines below, create analogies for classmates to complete. For ideas, use the word lists on pages 36–41, as well as a dictionary, thesaurus, or other reference materials.

1. _____ : _____ : : _____ : _____

    a. _____   c. _____

    b. _____   d. _____

2. _____ : _____ : : _____ : _____

    a. _____   c. _____

    b. _____   d. _____

3. _____ : _____ : : _____ : _____

    a. _____   c. _____

    b. _____   d. _____

4. _____ : _____ : : _____ : _____

    a. _____   c. _____

    b. _____   d. _____

5. _____ : _____ : : _____ : _____

    a. _____   c. _____

    b. _____   d. _____

Just for Fun: Choose one of the page titles in this book. Write an adventure story based on this title. Include in the story at least five of the words you used to complete analogies on that page. Underline these words in your story.

Analogy Word List
Synonyms

abrupt–sudden
adjust–fix
aid–assist
alone–solitary
anger–rage
answer–reply
arouse–awaken
beg–plead
blank–empty
brave–fearless
buy–purchase
calm–serene
caution–warn
choice–option
clear–plain
close–near
coarse–rough
coy–shy
danger–peril
decline–refuse
decrease–lessen
dense–thick
desire–want
detach–separate
disappear–vanish
divulge–disclose
dubious–doubtful
easy–simple
elect–choose
empty–vacant
enemy–rival
enormous–gigantic
extraordinary–unusual

false–untrue
fast–quick
fear–fright
fierce–ferocious
forgive–excuse
genuine–real
gleam–shine
govern–rule
grief–sorrow
guide–lead
happen–occur
hardy–strong
honest–sincere
hunt–seek
hurry–rush
identical–alike
ill–sick
imitate–copy
inquire–ask
late–tardy
leave–depart
liberty–freedom
limp–slack
marvelous–wonderful
meek–mild
mend–repair
merit–worth
misty–foggy
mix–blend
modern–recent
moist–damp
necessary–essential
need–require
nimble–spry

normal–ordinary
obvious–apparent
odor–smell
often–frequently
opinion–view
oppose–resist
pain–ache
peculiar–odd
petty–trivial
piece–part
promise–pledge
quiver–shake
reasonable–fair
recall–remember
refuse–decline
reimburse–repay
sensible–wise
severe–harsh
shiver–tremble
silly–foolish
small–tiny
task–job
teach–instruct
tease–taunt
tight–snug
timid–shy
tranquil–peaceful
useless–worthless
value–worth
verdict–judgment
whole–entire
worthy–honorable
zone–area

Analogy Word List
Antonyms

abate–increase
above–below
absent–present
accept–refuse
active–passive
advance–retreat
after–before
alike–different
allow–forbid
always–never
ambitious–lazy
appear–vanish
arrival–departure
ascent–descent
asleep–awake
attack–defend
back–front
beautiful–ugly
begin–end
believe–doubt
beneficial–harmful
best–worst
bold–timid
bottom–top
bright–dull
busy–idle
calm–excited
cheerful–somber
clean–dirty
close–open
cold–hot
common–rare
complex–simple
comply–resist

crooked–straight
dark–light
day–night
decrease–increase
deep–shallow
defeat–victory
difficult–easy
down–up
dry–wet
early–late
easy–hard
empty–full
evil–good
exact–vague
exterior–interior
fail–succeed
false–true
fancy–plain
far–near
fast–slow
first–last
flimsy–solid
foe–friend
foolish–wise
forget–remember
fragile–sturdy
fresh–stale
give–take
guilty–innocent
happy–sad
hard–soft
healthy–sick
heavy–light
high–low

include–omit
inferior–superior
irregular–regular
join–separate
joy–grief
kind–cruel
large–small
leave–stay
long–short
loose–tight
lose–win
many–few
maximum–minimum
nadir–zenith
narrow–wide
noisy–quiet
off–on
offense–defense
often–seldom
part–whole
permanent–temporary
plentiful–scarce
polite–rude
poor–rich
pull–push
rough–smooth
save–spend
short–tall
shrink–swell
start–stop
strong–weak
tame–wild
thick–thin
unusual–usual

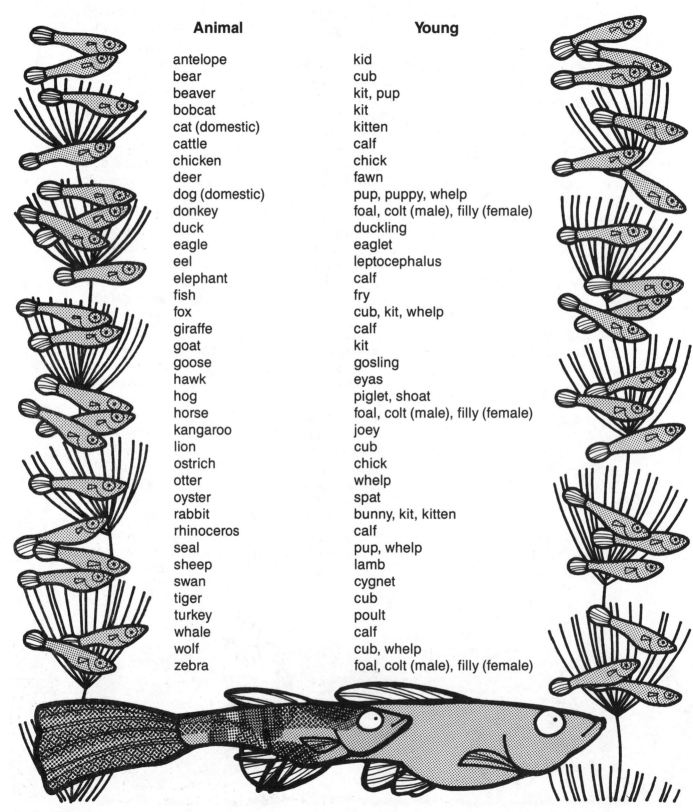

Analogy Word List
Animal Offspring

Animal	Young
antelope	kid
bear	cub
beaver	kit, pup
bobcat	kit
cat (domestic)	kitten
cattle	calf
chicken	chick
deer	fawn
dog (domestic)	pup, puppy, whelp
donkey	foal, colt (male), filly (female)
duck	duckling
eagle	eaglet
eel	leptocephalus
elephant	calf
fish	fry
fox	cub, kit, whelp
giraffe	calf
goat	kit
goose	gosling
hawk	eyas
hog	piglet, shoat
horse	foal, colt (male), filly (female)
kangaroo	joey
lion	cub
ostrich	chick
otter	whelp
oyster	spat
rabbit	bunny, kit, kitten
rhinoceros	calf
seal	pup, whelp
sheep	lamb
swan	cygnet
tiger	cub
turkey	poult
whale	calf
wolf	cub, whelp
zebra	foal, colt (male), filly (female)

Analogy Word List
Animal Groups

a **bevy** of larks or quail

a **brood** of birds

a **cast** of hawks

a **cete** of badgers

a **clowder** of cats

a **clutch** of chicks

a **colony** of ants, beavers, or rabbits

a **covert** of coots

a **covey** of partridges or quail

a **drift** of hogs

a **drove** of pigs or sheep

a **fall** of woodcocks

a **flight** of birds

a **flock** of chickens or goats

a **gaggle** of geese

a **gam** of whales

a **gang** of buffalo or elk

a **herd** of cattle, elephants, or horses

a **hive** of bees

a **muster** of peacocks

a **nide** of pheasants

a **pack** of dogs or wolves

a **pod** of seals or whales

a **pride** of lions

a **rafter** of turkeys

a **school** of fish

a **shoal** of fish or whales

a **skulk** of foxes

a **sloth** of bears

a **sord** of mallards

a **swarm** of bees

a **troop** of kangaroos or monkeys

Analogy Word List
Birds

adjutant
albatross
anhinga
auk
avocet
bird of paradise
bittern
bluebird
bobolink
bobwhite
booby
bowerbird
brant
cahow
cardinal
cassowary
cedar waxwing
chat
chickadee
chicken
cockatoo
cock of the rock
coly
condor
coot
cormorant
courser
crow
cuckoo
curlew
dipper
dodo
dove
duck
eagle
egret
emu
falcon
flamingo
flicker
flycatcher
frogmouth

goldfinch
goose
goshawk
grebe
grosbeak
guinea fowl
gull
hawk
heron
honey guide
hornbill
hummingbird
ibis
jackdaw
jay
kea
kestrel
killdeer
kingfisher
kiwi
kookaburra
loon
lorikeet
lovebird
lyrebird
macaw
magpie
marabou
meadowlark
mockingbird
myna
nightingale
nightjar
nuthatch
oriole
osprey
ostrich
ovenbird
owl
oyster catcher
parakeet
parrot
partridge

peafowl
pelican
penguin
petrel
pheasant
pigeon
puffin
quail
quetzal
rail
raven
rhea
roadrunner
robin
secretary bird
skua
skylark
sparrow
spoonbill
starling
stork
sunbird
swallow
swan
swift
tailorbird
tanager
tern
thrush
tinamou
toucan
touraco
towhee
trogon
turkey
vulture
warbler
weaverbird
whippoorwill
whydah
woodpecker
wren

Analogy Word List
Mammals

aardvark
addax
anteater
armadillo
aye-aye
baboon
badger
bat
bear
beaver
bison
camel
capybara
caracal
cat (domestic)
chamois
cheetah
chimpanzee
chinchilla
chipmunk
civet
coati
coyote
deer
dik-dik
dog (domestic)
eland
elephant
fox
galago
gerbil
gerenuk
gibbon

giraffe
gnu
gopher
gorilla
hamster
hartebeest
hedgehog
hippopotamus
horse
hyena
hyrax
ibex
jackal
jaguar
kangaroo
kinkajou
klipspringer
koala
lemming
lemur
leopard
lion
llama
lynx
manatee
markhor
marmoset
mink
mole
mongoose
moose
mouse
musk-ox

ocelot
okapi
opossum
orangutan
otter
panda
pangolin
peccary
platypus
porcupine
prairie dog
rabbit
raccoon
rhinoceros
seal
shrew
skunk
sloth
squirrel
tapir
thylacine
tiger
walrus
warthog
weasel
whale
wolf
wolverine
wombat
woodchuck
yak
zebra
zebu

Analogy Whizo Game
Instructions for the Teacher

1. Make one copy of the Analogy Whizo Word List on page 43 and one copy of the Analogy Whizo Game Card on page 44 for each player.

2. Distribute copies of the list and card to all players.

3. Tell players to prepare their playing cards by writing one word from the list in each box on the card. Caution them to select words from the list at random and to cross off each word as they use it so that no word will appear on any game card more than once.

4. Distribute markers of some kind, such as beans, paper clips, or squares of scrap paper, or make certain that each player has a sharpened pencil.

5. Tell players that they are to listen carefully as you read the first three terms of a four-term analogy. If a word on their card completes the analogy, they are to place a marker on the box containing that word or to use the pencil to draw an **X** through the box.

6. Slowly, read each of the analogies listed below in the following form:

give is to take as wet is to [pause]

Do *not* read the last word. Instead, pause to give players an opportunity to think of the answer and then to find and mark it on their cards. The last word has been listed so that you can check answers before you declare the winner.

7. The first player to mark five correct boxes in a row, whether vertically, horizontally, or diagonally, calls out, "Whizo!" If his answers are correct, he is declared the winner.

8. For variety, play Four-Corner Whizo, L Whizo, T Whizo, X Whizo, or Blackout Whizo, but remember to declare which variation of Whizo you are going to play *before* playing the game.

Four-Corner Whizo

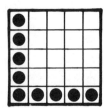

L Whizo

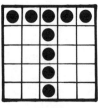

T Whizo

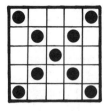

X Whizo

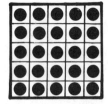

Blackout Whizo

Analogies to be Read Aloud

To further vary the game outcome, vary the order in which you read these analogies. For example, start with the right-hand rather than the left-hand column or read from bottom to top, rather than from top to bottom.

give : take :: wet : dry	clock : time :: thermometer : temperature	elect : choose :: tight : snug
lead : pencil :: ink : pen	flower : petal :: book : page	kid : goat :: fawn : deer
oriole : bird :: tulip : flower	salt : pepper :: bride : groom	victory : defeat :: polite : rude
buy : sell :: true : false	maximum : minimum :: tame : wild	adjust : fix :: calm : serene
checkers : game :: hockey : sport	empty : vacant :: damp : moist	physician : stethoscope :: barber : scissors
school : teacher :: hospital : doctor	sheep : lamb :: bear : cub	cod : fish :: magpie : bird
guilty : innocent :: joy : sorrow	chicken : flock :: wolf : pack	peril : danger :: veracity : truth
vanish : disappear :: rush : hurry	Miami : Florida :: Los Angeles : California	ruby : red :: lavender : purple
high : low :: many : few	rudder : ship :: steering wheel : truck	aunt : uncle :: niece : nephew
wealthy : rich :: skinny : thin	paprika : spice :: turquoise : color	final : last :: assist : aid
woman : lady :: lad : boy	fierce : ferocious :: imitate : copy	smooth : rough :: forget : remember
feather : soft :: rock : hard	quail : bird :: grasshopper : insect	pull : push :: save : spend

Analogy Whizo Word List

Instructions: Choose twenty-four words from the thirty-six words listed below. Write one word you have chosen in each box on the Analogy Whizo Card on page 44. As you choose your words, skip around. Do not simply copy them in order. Cross off each word you choose so that you will not write a word on your card more than once.

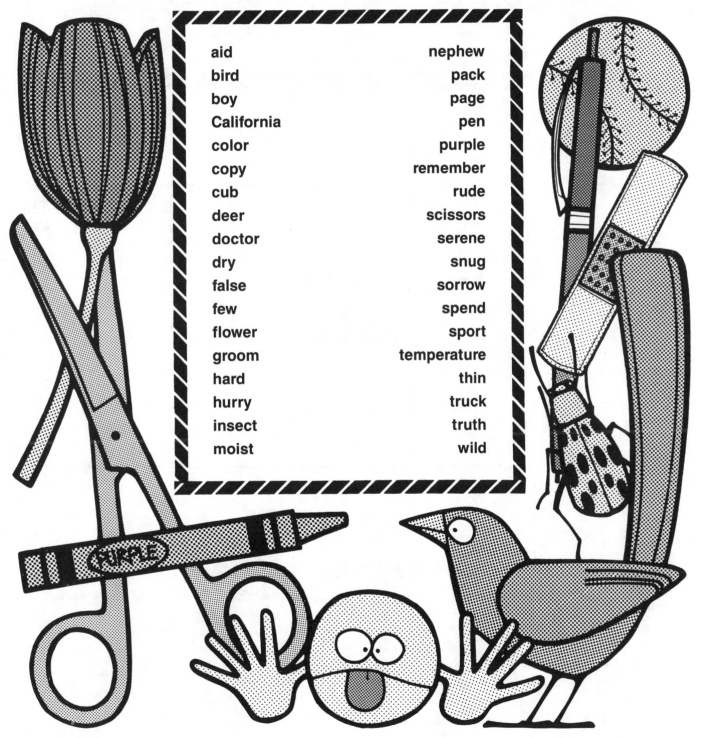

aid	nephew
bird	pack
boy	page
California	pen
color	purple
copy	remember
cub	rude
deer	scissors
doctor	serene
dry	snug
false	sorrow
few	spend
flower	sport
groom	temperature
hard	thin
hurry	truck
insect	truth
moist	wild

Analogy Whizo Game Card

Instructions: First, write one word from the list on page 43 in each of the boxes below except the box marked **free**. Next, listen carefully as your teacher reads an analogy. Then, if the word needed to complete that analogy is on your card, cover it with a marker or place an **x** in the square with it. When you have covered or marked five squares in a row horizontally, vertically, or diagonally, call out "Whizo!" The first player to do so wins the game.

		FREE		

WHIZO!

Adventure Score Chart

For each page, color one box for each analogy you completed correctly.

Number Correct	Page Number	9	10	11	12	13	14	15	16	17	18	19	20	21	22	23	24	25	26	27	28	29	30	31	32	33
10																										
9																										
8																										
7																										
6																										
5																										
4																										
3																										
2																										
1																										

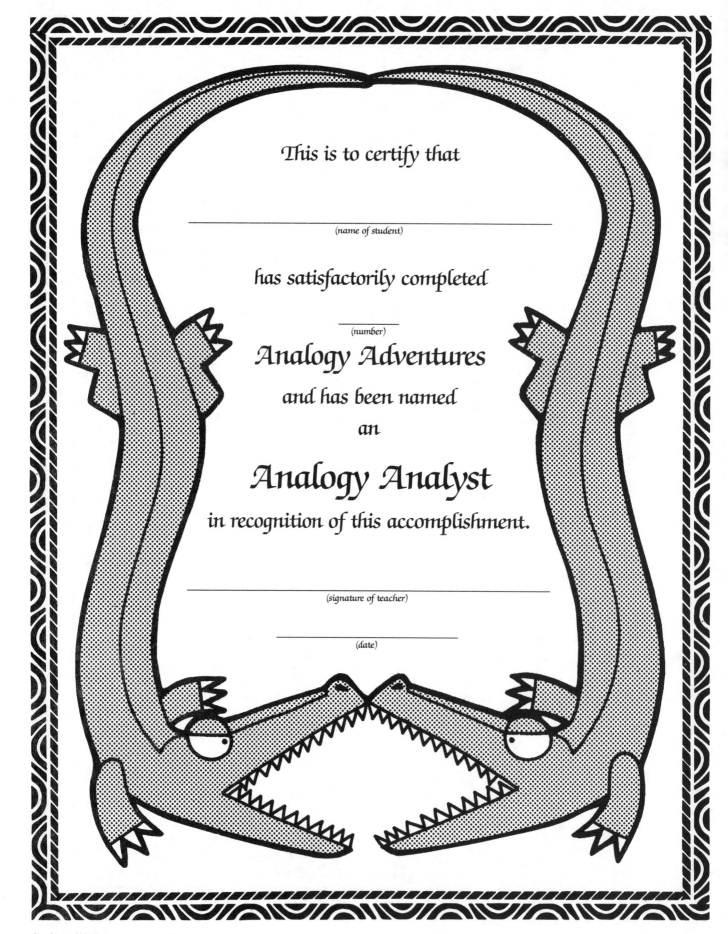

This is to certify that

_____
(name of student)

has satisfactorily completed

_____
(number)

Analogy Adventures

and has been named

an

Analogy Analyst

in recognition of this accomplishment.

_____
(signature of teacher)

_____
(date)

Answer Key

Page 7, Analogy Practice

1. antonyms, d. stupid
2. antonyms, d. ugly
3. homophones, a. flour
4. synonyms, d. shy

Page 8, More Analogy Practice

1. d. shirt
2. c. salmon
3. a. blue
4. c. turkeys
5. b. fish
6. a. astronomer
7. c. mare
8. synonyms, c. prison
9. antonyms, b. disapproving

Page 9, Balloon Bonanza

1. b. cold
2. c. leather
3. a. sink
4. d. liquid
5. b. water
6. c. grass
7. a. air
8. c. north
9. b. latch
10. d. coat

Page 10, Jungle Journey

1. b. automobile
2. a. slither
3. c. flower
4. d. tree
5. b. cold
6. c. vine
7. a. author
8. b. hear
9. d. whistle
10. c. desert

Page 11, Food Fantasy

1. a. sweet
2. b. daisy
3. c. pitcher
4. b. meatballs
5. b. male
6. b. groom
7. d. vegetable
8. d. tomato
9. b. flower
10. a. beverage

Page 12, Safari Sampler

1. d. thick
2. b. plead
3. b. chick
4. d. pray
5. d. retreat
6. b. kangaroo
7. b. fish
8. c. reptiles
9. d. rabbit
10. b. clothes

Page 13, Farm Fun

1. a. cub
2. b. feathers
3. c. deer
4. d. goose
5. a. dogs
6. c. duckling
7. b. crow
8. a. dew
9. d. wing
10. c. ox

Page 14, River Raft Revenge

1. a. hill
2. d. air
3. b. deep
4. a. female
5. c. temperature
6. c. bird
7. b. dry
8. b. fish
9. d. hard
10. a. mammals

Page 15, Sports Spectacular

1. c. soccer
2. a. cast
3. c. tuna
4. b. hockey
5. a. boxing
6. c. tennis
7. b. bowl
8. c. game
9. c. sad
10. a. alley

Page 16, Mountain Mania

1. b. few
2. d. trail
3. c. tramp
4. d. water
5. d. veil
6. d. trim
7. d. occur
8. c. plants
9. a. cave
10. c. come

Page 17, Museum Mystery

1. b. music
2. c. swipe
3. d. vanish
4. d. worth
5. a. conductor
6. c. red
7. d. palette
8. b. mystery
9. b. color
10. a. book

Page 18, Pirate Peril

1. b. pledge
2. a. car
3. d. writer
4. a. bag
5. d. riches
6. a. bow
7. c. mast
8. b. navel
9. c. group
10. b. crossbones

Page 19, Aerospace Adventure

1. b. car
2. b. end
3. c. peddle
4. b. caution
5. d. rigid
6. c. planet
7. d. turbulent
8. c. odometer
9. b. disembark
10. b. chicken

Page 20, Carnival Caper

1. d. vacation
2. d. trick
3. b. body
4. c. playful
5. a. drink
6. a. cart
7. b. rings
8. d. souvenir
9. d. night
10. a. choir

Page 21, Monster Mash

1. d. blend
2. b. whale
3. c. small
4. a. mice
5. d. soothe
6. b. lion
7. c. human
8. d. building
9. a. cowardly
10. b. hand

Page 22, Scuba Scare

1. c. pelican
2. a. beech
3. a. dirty
4. b. concealed
5. b. reef
6. d. tube
7. b. continent
8. a. biped
9. c. solid
10. b. belief

Answer Key
(continued)

Page 23, Rodeo Roundup

1. c. cow
2. d. rope
3. a. weak
4. b. deer
5. d. legs
6. c. pen
7. d. farmer
8. c. mane
9. c. laboratory
10. d. pack

Page 24, Gold Rush

1. a. carrot
2. b. fix
3. d. recluse
4. c. load
5. b. money
6. d. weighed
7. b. gallon
8. d. luster
9. b. far
10. b. counterfeit

Page 25, Explore Galore

1. b. probe
2. a. abundant
3. c. prints
4. b. for
5. d. North America
6. c. isthmus
7. a. damp
8. d. rebellion
9. c. oars
10. b. freight

Page 26, Gone Fishing

1. a. dove
2. d. stale
3. c. meter
4. c. trout
5. d. vague
6. b. fast
7. c. idle
8. c. food
9. d. truck
10. d. trivial

Page 27, Jam Session

1. d. trumpet
2. b. pickle
3. d. waltz
4. a. down
5. b. nose
6. c. polite
7. b. rhythm
8. b. cord
9. b. bass
10. c. see

Page 28, Taste Treat

1. a. ambrosia : coconut
2. c. toucan : oriole
3. c. knead : dough
4. b. ounce : cup
5. b. poach : fish
6. c. drake : duck
7. d. skin : peach
8. a. obvious : clear
9. a. beige : khaki
10. b. Madrid : Spain

Page 29, Amazing Amusements

1. a. Ferris wheel : carnival
2. b. listen : tape
3. c. Hansel : Gretel
4. a. bugle : blow
5. c. mankind : anthropologist
6. b. bow : archery
7. c. implication : suggestion
8. a. aquarium : fish
9. b. entomologist : insects
10. b. solo : one

Page 30, Science Sensation

1. a. antelope : kid
2. a. amusement : entertainment
3. d. test : hypothesis
4. c. decibel : sound
5. c. viola : instrument
6. d. wheel : spoke
7. d. sty : pig
8. c. Richter : earthquakes
9. c. method : technique
10. c. meteorologist : weather

Page 31, Anatomy Ambush

1. c. attack : assault
2. b. elbow : arm
3. c. fingers : snap
4. d. nail : finger
5. a. drum : ear
6. c. nape : neck
7. a. femur : leg
8. a. gills : water
9. b. relax : tighten
10. b. digest : stomach

Page 32, Sly Spy

1. b. furtive : stealthy
2. d. sleuth : investigator
3. b. open : overt
4. a. insect : beetle
5. d. yacht : sloop
6. d. zeal : fervor
7. d. screwdriver : tool
8. d. unify : unite
9. c. previous : prior
10. c. imprison : liberate

Page 33, Daredevil Dynamo

1. c. foolhardy : rash
2. d. trick : stunt
3. a. cyclone : typhoon
4. c. hero : heroine
5. b. fathom : depth
6. b. prolong : extend
7. b. brave : cowardly
8. d. russet : brown
9. a. ambitious : lofty
10. a. century : hundred